A Tail
of
Two Lakes

ISBN 979-8-89112-602-2 (Paperback)
ISBN 979-8-89112-603-9 (Digital)

Covenant Books
11661 Hwy 707
Murrells Inlet, SC 29576
www.covenantbooks.com

A Tail
of
Two Lakes

A Story of Loss, Grief, and Healing

by J. L. Garrett

In the year of the King Fisher, the fish filled the waters and they were of many different forms. Of all the fish, there was one very different and special. Her name was Frizzy the gold fish. She lived in a beautiful lake in the land where the clouds light up the moon, and everyone understands that clouds really do have silver linings.

Frizzy was different from other fish. Most fish just swim around in schools following the tail in front of them. Frizzy loved other things in the lake, not just fish.

Everything in the lake was a part of her family.
First, there was Auntie Bullfrog.

She just loved the way Auntie could jump around the lake.

Then there was Uncle Spoony Mooney the raccoon.

She loved to watch him wash his food in the lake,
which he did all the time.

There was also a squirrel named Squireley Pearly, whom Frizzy watched leap from limb to limb in the tops of the trees. All these were a part of her family.

Frizzy thought she knew everyone in the lake. Then one day, she was delighted down to the very tippies of her gills to see another fish she had never seen before. He was big and moved quite slow, and had this silly grin that went from gill to gill.

His name was Pokey the Big-Mouthed Bass.
Frizzy and Pokey hit it right off. Even though
they were fish of a different color, they soon fell
in love with each other.

Not long after Frizzy and Pokey fell in love, they had Huggy and Angel. Two beautiful little children that they loved very much.

It was wonderful to swim around the lake together, and Frizzy and Pokey introduced Huggy and Angel to all their friends.

In this lake, there was a legend about a great bird called the King Fisher. Pokey and Frizzy talked a lot about the King Fisher. Many of the fish in the lake didn't believe there was such a thing; others were afraid of the King Fisher. They had friends who had simply disappeared while swimming close to the water's surface. Frizzy and Pokey knew the King Fisher was real. They were not too afraid of him. They had seen him fly over the lake and were awed by his beauty.

Pokey actually spoke to the King Fisher one day. He saw him in a great mustard tree by the side of the lake. They soon became good friends, and Pokey would go every day to talk.

The King Fisher told Pokey of a great lake far away and of the beauty of swimming in its deep waters.

Pokey asked if it were possible for him to see the lake? The King Fisher told him he could take him there, but he would never be able to come back to the lake with Auntie Bullfrog, Spoony Moony, Squireley Pearly, Huggy, Angel, or Frizzy. Pokey didn't really want to go. He didn't want to leave Frizzy or Huggy or Angel or anyone else in the lake.

The more Pokey thought about that beautiful, clear, deep lake, the more he knew he was going to be swimming in it. Frizzy didn't know that Pokey thought he might end up swimming in that great lake. Soon Pokey swam to the surface of the lake, and the great King Fisher gently grasped him, and he was gone.

Frizzy did not understand what had happened. Pokey was gone, and the lake seemed empty and small. The lake didn't seem the same.

After Pokey was gone, the skies opened up. Lightning flashed, and thunder roared across the lake. Frizzy, Huggy, and Angel had never seen it rain like this before.

The water began to rise, and the waves were huge with the wind blowing them into a froth. Frizzy, Angel, and Huggy were being pushed along by the rising water. They tried to swim against it, but it was too strong. The lake rose so high, the water began to be pushed off a cliff into a waterfall!

Frizzy, Huggy, and Angel tried as hard as they could to swim against the current but found themselves going over the waterfall!

The water was so wild, they could not see each other, and Angel and Huggy were terrified they had lost Frizzy.

Soon they found themselves in a swift-moving stream dodging large rocks and tree limbs. After awhile, the water slowed and became more clear. Suddenly they could see Frizzy up ahead of them and were so relieved they had not lost her. They were able to swim together again even though they still had to dodge and swim around rocks and branches.

They were getting good at dealing with the strong current and even began to enjoy moving with the current and quickly going around whatever blocked their path.

Finally after what seemed forever, the water slowed. Soon Frizzy, Angel, and Huggy found theselves in a new and strange lake where they had never been. Everything looked different.

Nothing looked normal. Huge cedar trees lined the lake and seemed to rise all the way to the mountaintops.

Frizzy, Angel, and Huggy really missed Pokey. Frizzy was sad that Pokey was gone. She was also mad at him for leaving. One day, Frizzy looked up into a huge cedar tree and saw the King Fisher there! She talked to the King Fisher about being angry at Pokey for leaving. She wanted to go back to the old lake but knew they could not do it. Frizzy talked to the King Fisher about feeling left behind.

This new lake is so different. It is really deep. The King Fisher said, "It is good that you now have a need to swim deeper."

Huggy didn't understand about needing to swim deeper. He swam as deep as he could, but he still missed Pokey. He was angry that Pokey was gone and everything had changed. He wondered if Pokey had gone because of him. He was angry at the King Fisher and would not talk to him. He did find someone else to talk to on a log at the edge of the lake. It was Slippery Snake. He was a big shiny beautiful snake. He lay on the log in the sun all day to warm himself. Huggy talked to Slippery about losing Pokey and being angry at the King Fisher. Slippery Snake said he was sorry for Huggy's loss, and it was most certainly the King Fisher's fault.

Slippery Snake told Huggy any time he wanted to come talk, he would be glad to come close and listen. Huggy thanked him but didn't feel like talking anymore and swam off to be alone.

Frizzy saw Huggy talking to Slippery Snake and told him he should not get to close to him, but Huggy didn't want to listen. Soon after,

Huggy went to talk to Slippery Snake about how lonely he felt. Slippery Snake said, "Come closer so I can comfort you." Huggy felt a little uncomfortable, but he moved closer to Slippery Snake. As soon as he was close, Slippery Snake opened his mouth, showing his long sharp teeth and with an awful look in his eyes and a smile on his face leaped at Huggy with his poisonous fangs pointed straight at Huggy.

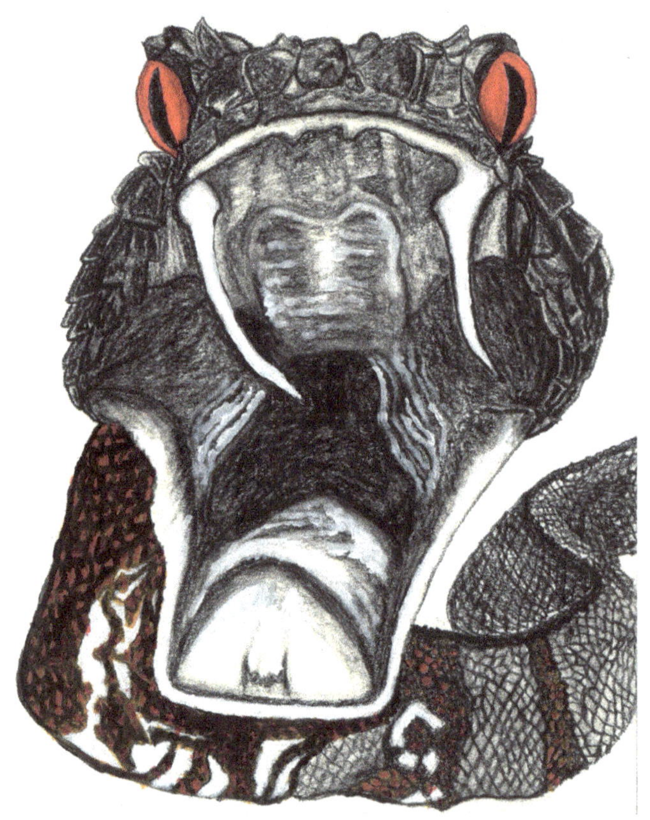

At that very moment, there was a flash of blue in the air as the King Fisher grasped Slippery Snake in midair before he could kill Huggy. The King Fisher and Slipppery Snake flew up into the sky grasping, clawing, and fighting all the way. It was a terrible fight with Slippery Snake wrapping himself around the King Fisher. The last thing Huggy saw was Slippery Snake sticking his fangs into the side of the King Fisher and both falling into the forest.

Huggy realized that the King Fisher had just saved his life. After that time, they thought they saw the King Fisher high in the sky. They could hear his song floating over the lake and through the forest. Whenever they heard the King Fisher's song, they felt joyful and at peace. It made them feel safe and loved. They did not see the King Fisher, but they heard his song all the time. It rang through the mountains, through the forest, and over the lake with its beautiful sound.

Huggy was confused at first, but he felt better now. He didn't swim alone anymore. He found new friends that he loved to swim and play with in the lake and learned to swim deep with them. The whole lake became his playground, and he wasn't afraid to explore and try new things, and he could always hear the song of the King Fisher.

If I take the wings of the morning and
dwell in the uttermost parts of the sea,
even there your hand shall lead me,
and your right hand shall hold me.
—Psalm 139:9–10 (RSV)

For you have been my help, and in the
shadow of your wings I will sing for joy.
—Psalm 63:7 (RSV)

About the Author

J. L. Garrett has spent over thirty years helping people through physical and emotional loss as a United Methodist pastor and licensed physical therapist. His experience involved conducting grief and divorce recovery seminars, as well as working with those who have had loss of physical abilities. This book, *A Tail of Two Lakes*, evolved out of a grief seminar with the hope of helping children with loss and grief.

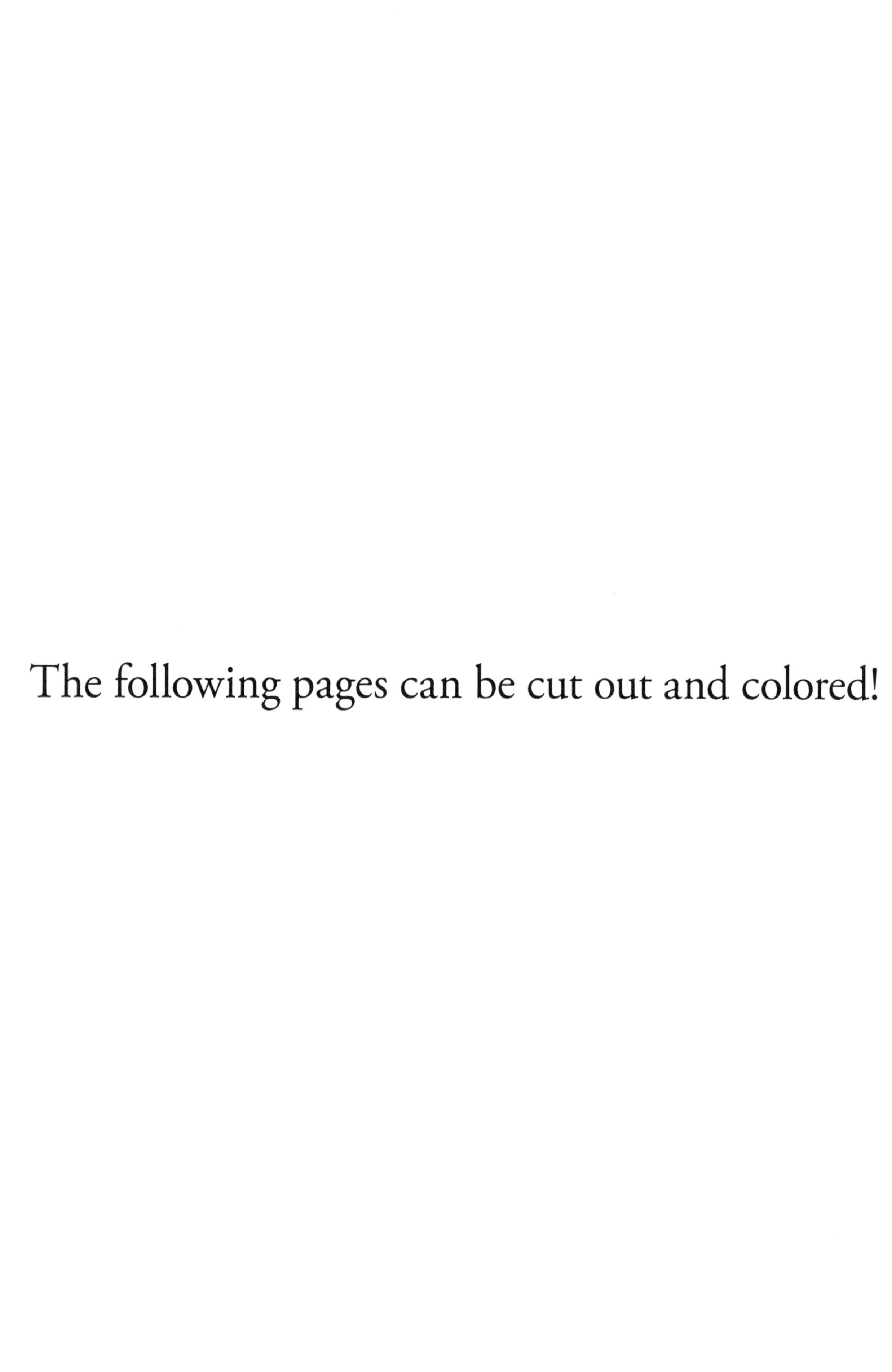

The following pages can be cut out and colored!

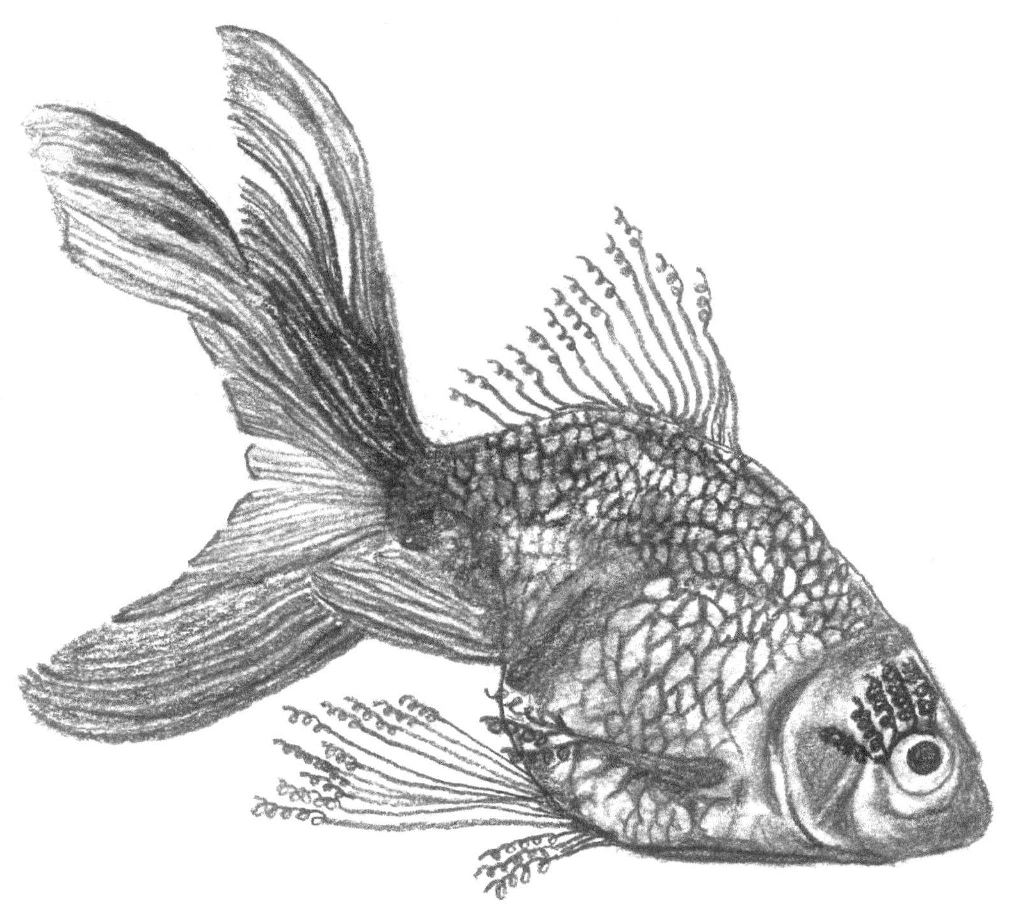

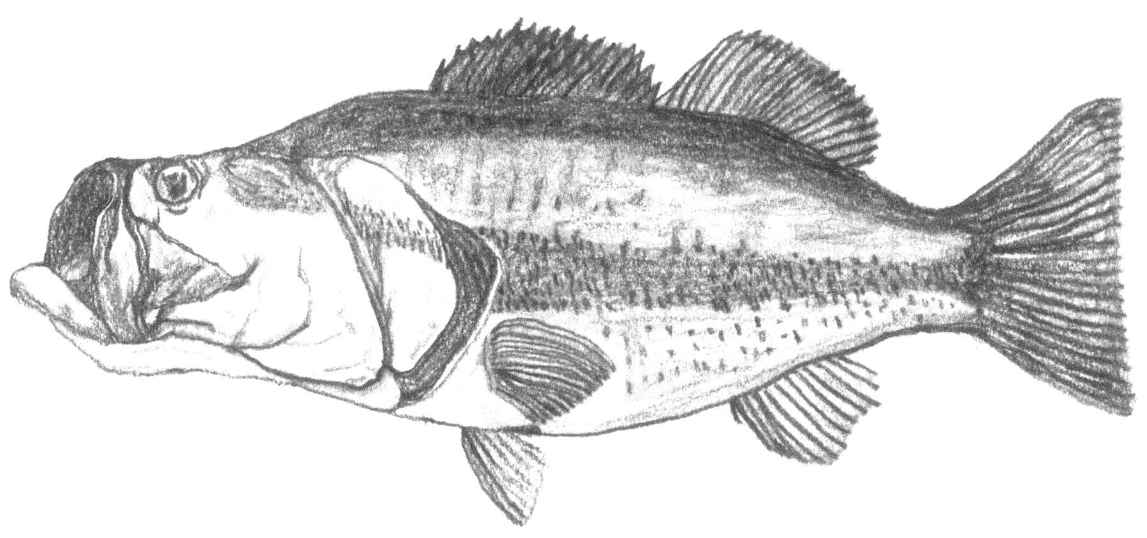

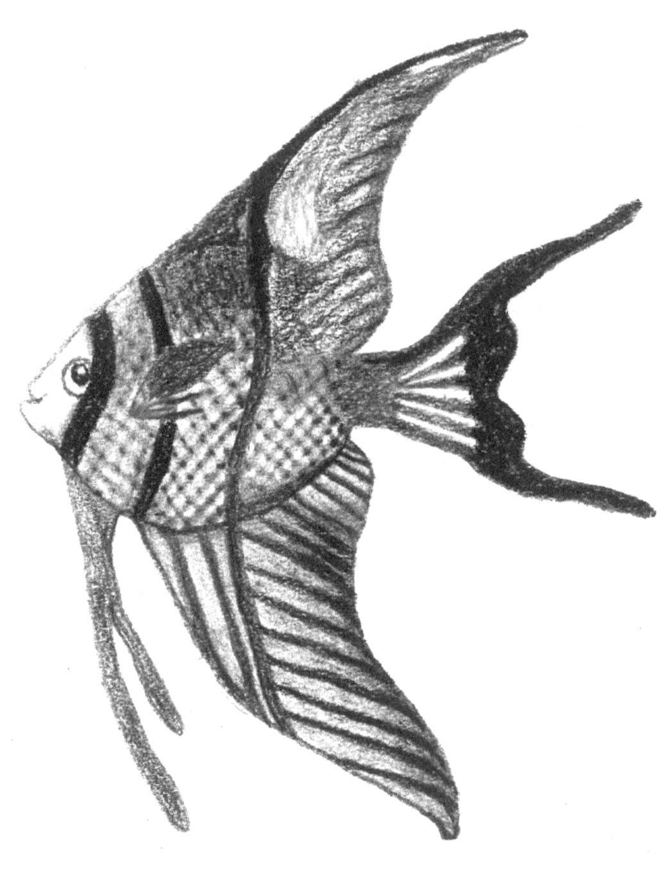

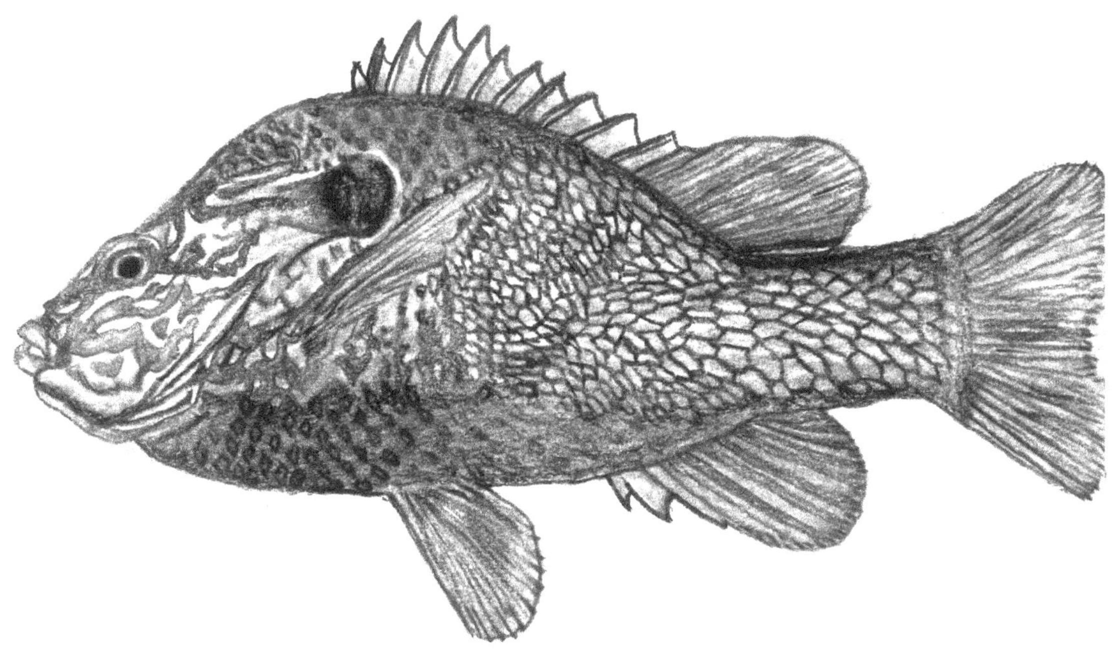

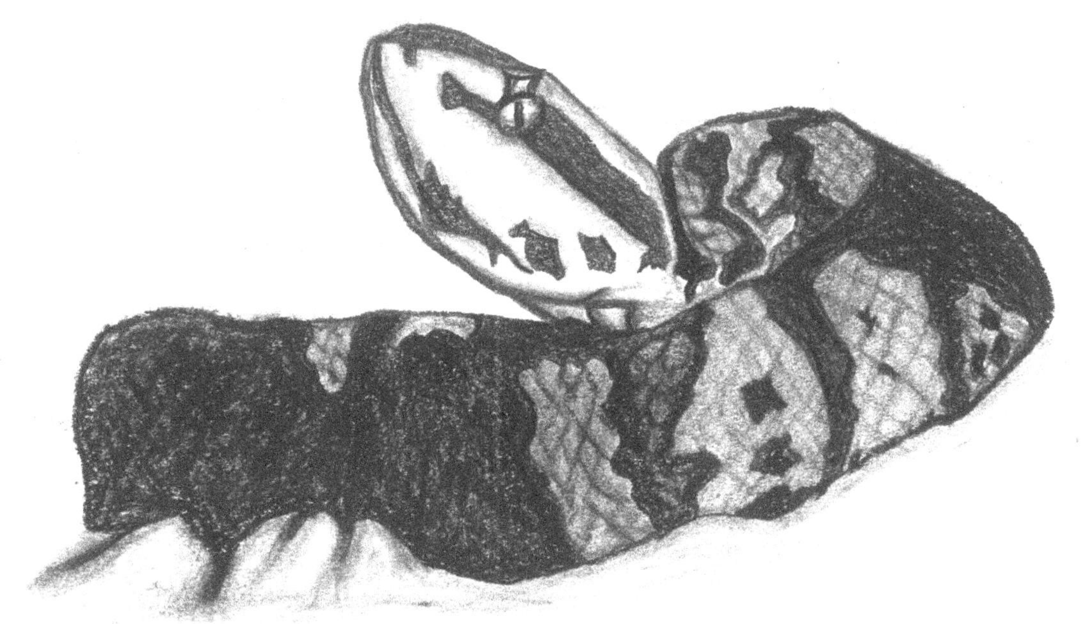

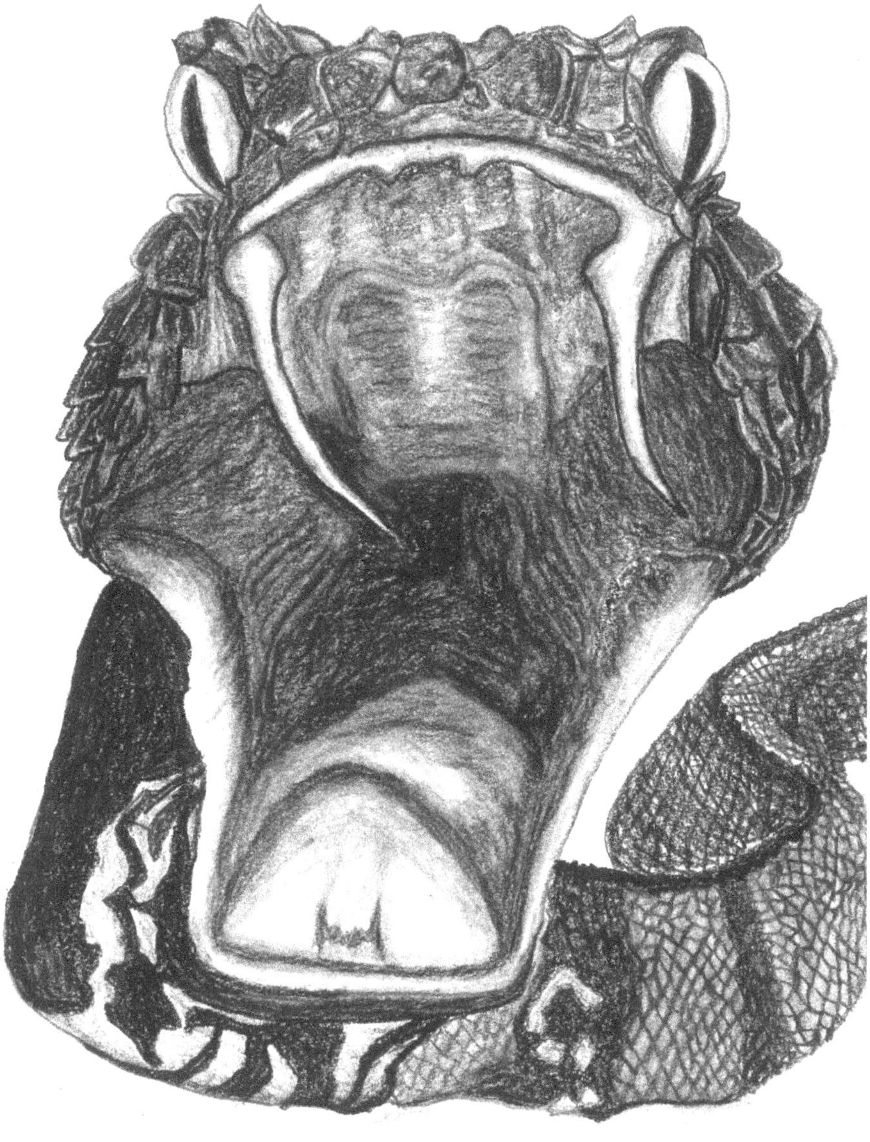